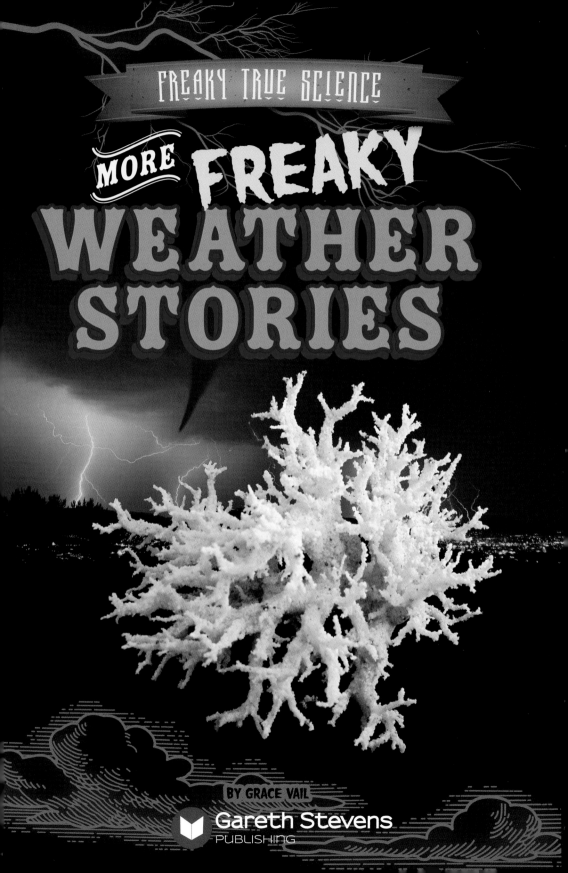

FREAKY TRUE SCIENCE

MORE FREAKY WEATHER STORIES

BY GRACE VAIL

Gareth Stevens
PUBLISHING

Please visit our website, www.garethstevens.com. For a free color catalog of all our high-quality books, call toll free 1-800-542-2595 or fax 1-877-542-2596.

Cataloging-in-Publication Data

Names: Vail, Grace, author.
Title: More freaky weather stories / Grace Vail.
Other titles: Freaky weather stories | Freaky true science.
Description: New York : Gareth Stevens Publishing, [2020] | Series: Freaky true science | Includes bibliographical reference and index.
Identifiers: LCCN 2019005525| ISBN 9781538240748 (pbk.) | ISBN 9781538240762 (library bound) | ISBN 9781538240755 (6 pack)
Subjects: LCSH: Weather–Miscellanea–Juvenile literature. | Weather forecasting–Juvenile literature. | Natural disasters–Juvenile literature.
Classification: LCC QC981.3 .V35 2020 | DDC 551.5–dc23
LC record available at https://lccn.loc.gov/2019005525

First Edition

Published in 2020 by
Gareth Stevens Publishing
111 East 14th Street, Suite 349
New York, NY 10003

Copyright © 2020 Gareth Stevens Publishing

Designer: Sarah Liddell
Editor: Therese Shea

Photo credits: Cover, p. 1 (lightning bolt) Potapov Alexander/Shutterstock.com; cover, p. 1 (cloud used throughout book) Mila Petkova/Shutterstock.com; cover, p. 1 (storm) swa182/Shutterstock.com; cover, p. 1 (fulgurite) yoyoj3d1/Fickr.com; background throughout book leedsn/Shutterstock.com; hand used throughout Helena Ohman/Shutterstock.com; paper texture used throughout Alex Gontar/Shutterstock.com; p. 5 James BO Insogna/Shutterstock.com; p. 7 Darkfoxelixir/Shutterstock.com; p. 9 Wild Horizon/Contributor/Universal Images Group/Getty Images; p. 11 Dex Sightseeing Photography/Shutterstock.com; p. 13 vincent noel/Shutterstock.com; p. 15 christianpinillo/Shutterstock.com; p. 17 REDA&CO/Contributor/Universal Images Group/Getty Images; p. 18 Originalwana/Wikimedia Commons; p. 19 reisegraf.ch/Shutterstock.com; p. 21 Matilda Anderson/Shutterstock.com; p. 22 Jochos89/Wikimedia Commons; p. 23 Rvagg/Wikimedia Commons; p. 25 Saperaud~commonswiki/Wikimedia Commons; p. 27 Designua/Shutterstock.com; p. 29 OceanAtoll/Wikimedia Commons.

Printed in the United States of America

CONTENTS

Words in the glossary appear in **bold** type
the first time they are used in the text.

WEIRD WEATHER

Sometimes, weather can be unusual. It can do things that surprise us, confuse us, and even wow us. Usually, meteorologists understand why weather happens. They use this knowledge to predict the kind of weather events we can expect. Their forecasts can help us plan our lives. But there are times when strange and unexpected weather occurs.

Weird weather events can be caused by any number of reasons. In this book, you'll learn about such cool weather **phenomena** as never-ending lightning storms, fog tsunamis, and really odd cloud

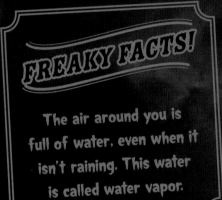

FREAKY FACTS!

The air around you is full of water, even when it isn't raining. This water is called water vapor.

formations. Some of these things are so strange that you may have never experienced or even heard of them! However, in learning about them, you'll understand more about weather in general. Are you ready to become an expert on freaky weather?

SOME TYPES OF WEATHER SUCH AS RAIN, SNOW, AND THUNDERSTORMS OCCUR IN OUR EVERYDAY LIVES. OTHER WEATHER EVENTS HAPPEN VERY RARELY!

WHAT IS A METEOROLOGIST?

A meteorologist is a person who studies weather, or the state of Earth's atmosphere. Meteorologists use their knowledge and observations to **predict** weather. However, predictions are challenging because weather can change very quickly for many reasons. Meteorologists use lots of instruments and kinds of **technology** to help them gather information about temperature, wind speed, air pressure, **humidity**, and more. The more data they can gather, the better their predictions will be.

5

MOONBOW MADNESS

Everyone loves to see a rainbow. Rainbows appear because of the refracting, or bending, of light in water droplets in the air. So, it makes sense that we see them when the sun comes out after a rainstorm. A similar event can occur in certain cases at night, resulting in a moonbow—a rainbow caused by moonlight!

In addition to needing a good amount of moisture in the air, the moon itself also needs to be nearly full so that it gives off enough light to create the phenomena. Similar to a rainbow, moonlight may be separated into different **wavelengths** in the water droplets. Longer wavelengths appear as red and orange to us, while shorter ones look like blue and purple.

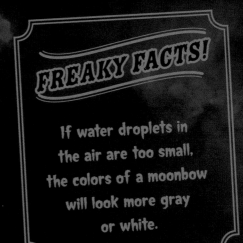

FREAKY FACTS!

If water droplets in the air are too small, the colors of a moonbow will look more gray or white.

CONDITIONS THAT CAUSE MOONBOWS

Many conditions must be just right in order to see a moonbow. First, you must be standing in the right spot. Also, a nearly full or full moon must be low in the sky, at a 42-degree angle or lower. Finally, there needs to be the right amount of moisture in the air so the light can refract in the right way. It makes sense why you don't see these more often, doesn't it?

LIGHTNING CAN DO WHAT?

What happens when lightning strikes the ground? If it strikes the right place, it can create glass out of minerals! That's right—glass—but not the kind of glass you have around your house. This is glass you can't see through. It's formed when particles of sand or rock are heated to extremely high temperatures by lightning. The particles are fused, or joined, into a glassy mineral formation called fulgurite. *Fulgur* is the Latin word for "lightning," and *–ite* is a word ending for minerals and rocks.

Sand fulgurites are the most common type. They're often shaped like cylinders, or tubes, and can reach lengths of more than 60 feet (18 m). Rock fulgurites, however, are more like a coating of thin glass on rocks. They may branch out like veins on a rock's surface.

FREAKY FACTS!

Lightning can heat the air around it to 50,000°F (27,760°C)!

WHERE TO LOOK

Certain places are especially good areas to search for fulgurites. Of course, sand fulgurites are made in sandy places, like beaches. The beaches of Lake Michigan and the coast of the Atlantic Ocean are likely places to find them. Mountain peaks also attract lightning. Rock fulgurites are found in the Rocky Mountains, the Sierra Nevada, and many other peaks. Fulgurites are a good reminder that these places are dangerous when lightning is striking!

YOU CAN CLEARLY SEE THE PATHWAY OF LIGHTNING THROUGH THIS FULGURITE MADE FROM QUARTZ SAND.

STRANGE TSUNAMIS

You probably know a bit about tsunamis. Underwater earthquakes or volcanic eruptions are the usual causes of these freaky huge waves. The energy from these violent natural events creates a series of waves that may not be that big at first. However, they pick up speed, traveling hundreds of miles per hour, and grow in height until they reach shallow waters. By then, the waves may be taller than a three-story building.

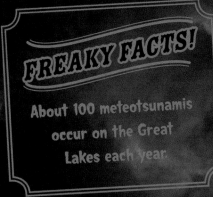

FREAKY FACTS!

About 100 meteotsunamis occur on the Great Lakes each year.

What is less known is that weather can cause tsunamis, too. Thunderstorms can be the cause of meteorological tsunamis, or meteotsunamis, because of the changes in wind and air pressure that accompany them. When a storm passes over water, it may create large waves that can travel great distances very swiftly.

METEOTSUNAMIS IN LAKE MICHIGAN

In April 2018, a storm caused two meteotsunamis in Lake Michigan. When the waves hit shore, they flooded the coast and broke docks. Luckily, no one was hurt. In 1954, a 10-foot (3 m) meteotsunami in Lake Michigan killed seven men fishing on a pier in Chicago, Illinois. Similar events have occurred on other lakes and bodies of water around the world. Since these waves travel far, it doesn't have to be stormy where the meteotsunami hits shore.

IN 2018, POWERFUL STORMS CAUSED A METEOTSUNAMI OFF THE COAST OF DELAWARE, SHOWN HERE. METEOTSUNAMIS ARE ALMOST IMPOSSIBLE TO PREDICT.

A FOG TSUNAMI?

Weather can sometimes trick our eyes and make us think we're seeing something that isn't actually happening. One example is a fog bank. It can look just like a tsunami! A fog bank occurs when warm air condenses, or changes from a gas to a liquid, over a cold body of water. Tiny water droplets are suspended in the air. This is what we see when we observe fog.

While fog can occur any time, we usually see fog banks in late spring or early summer when water temperatures are cold, but air temperatures begin to warm. When the fog bank that forms stretches wide and towers high above the water, it can give the startling appearance of a tsunami. Luckily, it's just scary to look at!

FREAKY FACTS!

The foggiest place in the world is Grand Banks, an area in the Atlantic Ocean near Newfoundland, Canada.

WHAT MAKES FOG DANGEROUS?

Fog is often pretty harmless. But it can actually be deadly sometimes—not because of what it's made up of, water vapor, but because of how it impairs our vision. When fog is thick, people who are driving cars can't see very far ahead of them. It's harder for them to see other cars or people in the road. Fog affects air travel, too. That's why airlines may delay flights until fog has passed to keep travelers safe.

A FOG BANK LIKE THE ONE SEEN HERE CAN LOOK REALLY TERRIFYING!

LONG, LONG LIGHTNING STORM

During a thunderstorm, you can sometimes hear thunder and see lightning. Imagine a lightning storm that's months long! There actually is one over Lake Maracaibo in Venezuela. The storm has a name—Relámpago del Catatumbo—which means "lightning of the Catatumbo." The Catatumbo is a nearby river. This weird weather occurs every night for 8 months of the year—about 40,000 lightning bolts per night. Even weirder, the storm takes place 3 miles (4.8 km) up in the sky. You can observe it from the ground, but you can't hear it!

There are a few different theories to explain the storm. One is that methane gas rises from the Catatumbo, mixes with cold, dry mountain air, and makes conditions right for lightning. Another is that the humidity and weather of the region spark the storm.

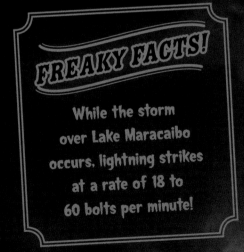

FREAKY FACTS!

While the storm over Lake Maracaibo occurs, lightning strikes at a rate of 18 to 60 bolts per minute!

THIS LIGHTNING STORM RAGES ON FOR MONTHS AND MONTHS, AND NO ONE REALLY KNOWS WHY YET!

HOW CLOSE IS YOUR LIGHTNING STORM?

Did you know you could find out how many miles away lightning struck? When you see a flash of lightning in the sky, count the number of seconds that pass until you hear a crack of thunder. Then take that number and divide it by 5. That's the distance of the lightning strike. For example, if you count 5 seconds between the lightning flash and the thunder, the lightning struck 1 mile (1.6 km) away.

15

ODD ICE FORMATIONS

In the Arctic and Antarctic Oceans, freezing temperatures cause a lot of different kinds of ice to form. Ice sheets, ice caps, and icebergs are some of the more recognized ice formations. But other formations are a bit stranger, like frost flowers!

These aren't real flowers, but they look much like flowers—or really big snowflakes. They occur when the air over the water is much colder than the water. The flowerlike formations appear thanks to sublimating ice, or ice that changes from a solid to a gas. When this gas becomes **saturated** with moisture, it changes to liquid. In very cold conditions, the liquid turns into frost. The frost grows around ice crystals, sometimes leading to the growth of unusual formations, such as frost flowers.

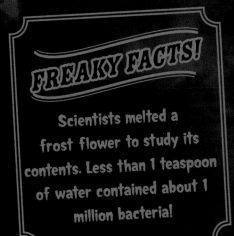

FREAKY FACTS!

Scientists melted a frost flower to study its contents. Less than 1 teaspoon of water contained about 1 million bacteria!

ICE FLOWERS

Ice formations can also occur directly on plants, and the results are cool! When the air is at a freezing temperature but the ground is warmer than the air, water can be drawn out of flower stems. It can freeze in the middle of the air, sometimes curling into amazing shapes too delicate to hold. This often happens at night. Once formed, ice flowers only last for a little while. They melt quickly on sunny days.

Penitentes are another odd ice creation. These spiky formations of snow or ice point up towards the sun. The process that causes these to form is similar to the formation of frost flowers—sublimation.

Penitentes don't just happen everywhere there's snow. They need special conditions to form, especially high altitudes. They're found in the glaciers of the Andes Mountains and in the Atacama Desert of Chile, for example, where the dry air and sunlight are just right for their formation.

This is how it works: Sunlight melts certain areas on a snowy surface, causing **depressions**. The shape of the depression changes the angle of sunlight hitting the surface, speeding up sublimation and causing the rising particles of water vapor to turn back into ice in the shape of a tower.

THESE SPIKY ICE FORMATIONS CAN GO ON FOR MILES. THE TALLEST PENITENTES REACH OVER 13 FEET (4 M) INTO THE AIR!

MAN-MADE PENITENTES

Scientists have created penitentes in a lab. They placed a block of icy snow in a freezer with a see-through top. They cooled the air, shined a light on the block, and created spikes in just a few hours. They found that increasing temperatures—those over 24°F (–4.4°C)—slowed growth. Changing humidity in the air didn't affect growth until it exceeded 70 percent. So, very humid air and warmer temperatures aren't good for the growth of penitentes.

COMPLICATED CLOUDS

When you look up at the sky on a sunny day, sometimes you can see puffy white clouds floating around. They can be quite beautiful—or kind of weird looking! They may appear like something other than clouds. Wave clouds, for example, look like waves cresting in the ocean. They occur when the air in the atmosphere is moving at two different speeds. The upper layer moves faster than the lower layer and pushes the different parts of the cloud until a wavelike shape forms.

Scientists sometimes call wave clouds by a different name—Kelvin Helmholtz clouds. "Kelvin" is for scientist Lord Kelvin and "Helmholtz" is for Hermann von Helmholtz, who both studied conditions that make this type of cloud possible.

FREAKY FACTS!

Some people think wave clouds were the inspiration for Vincent van Gogh's famous painting *The Starry Night!*

WHY DO CLOUDS FORM?

Clouds can be pretty cool, but why are they there? When you learned about fog tsunamis, you learned about condensation. A similar process is what makes clouds. When water **evaporates**, it rises up into the sky as the gas called water vapor. The water vapor cools as it rises into the atmosphere and condenses into water droplets or ice droplets, often around bits of dust and pollen. When enough of these particles gather together, they form clouds.

WHAT DO THESE COOL CLOUDS TELL US? THEY'RE OFTEN SIGNS THAT WEATHER IS CHANGING IN THE ATMOSPHERE. THEY ALSO MEAN THERE'S TURBULENT AIR UP THERE!

If wave clouds look odd, morning glory clouds look unnatural! These unusual clouds form in the sky in the shape of a tube. They can be really long, stretching for hundreds of miles across the sky.

A morning glory cloud is a solitary wave cloud—or a soliton. This means it has one crest and moves without changing speed or structure. Scientists have studied the formation of morning glory clouds near the peninsula of Cape York in Australia. They think the meeting of winds coming off the water from the east and west over this particular landform creates the special conditions that produce the astonishing morning glory clouds. If the air temperature, speed, and humidity are just right, sometimes as many as 10 form in a row!

FREAKY FACTS!

A morning glory cloud can be 600 miles (966 km) long!

CLOUDY DAYS AHEAD

Freaky clouds are fun to learn about, but what about those clouds we see every day? They form in different levels of Earth's atmosphere and have special shapes and names. They can tell us about the weather to come. For example, cotton-like formations called cumulus clouds tell us that the weather will be nice, while mountain-like clouds called cumulonimbus clouds tell us that rain, hail, and even **tornadoes** could be coming our way!

PILLAR POWER

Sunsets are some of the loveliest events in nature. If you're lucky, you might experience a sun pillar while watching a sunset. A sun pillar is a vertical ray of light that looks like it's reaching up or down from the sun. This occurs when tiny, flat, **hexagon**-shaped ice crystals float down from Earth's atmosphere horizontally, or parallel to the ground. The sun's rays reflect off them, causing us to see a sun pillar. This light formation is most often viewed at sunset or sunrise.

The moon and man-made lights can create pillars of light, too. These are called light pillars rather than sun pillars. If you don't think this is freaky, you should know that some light pillars look so strange that people have thought they're UFOs!

FREAKY FACTS!

Light pillars are sometimes seen over Niagara Falls. Light from the nearby city reflects off the mist from the waterfalls—creating a pillar of light!

WHAT TO EXPECT

Set your alarm! Sun pillars are easiest to see within a few minutes of sunrise or sunset. Although they may look like they're under or over the sun, the upper pillar—extending upward—is the one that's most often visible. At first, it has a similar color as the sun. However, it often changes from a light orange-white color to a darker orange-red. Sun pillars usually fade away within an hour of sunset.

HOLA, EL NIÑO!

Another weird feature of weather is that conditions on the ground can affect it. Did you know the ocean causes major weather events? One of these is called El Niño. That's the name for an unusually warm current in the Pacific Ocean near the west coast of South America. It changes weather patterns all over the world. It's brought rain to deserts and **drought** to normally rainy places.

El Niño doesn't have a regular schedule, but usually happens every 3 to 7 years. When it occurs, **trade winds** near the equator blowing from east to west grow weaker. So, warm waters that usually remain in the western Pacific Ocean move east, bringing rainstorms to areas near the central and eastern Pacific Ocean.

FREAKY FACTS!

La Niña is the opposite of El Niño: Trade winds strengthen, bringing unusually cold waters to the eastern and central Pacific Ocean and unusual weather conditions to different parts of the world.

UNEXPECTED EFFECTS

El Niño has more effects than unusual wet and dry weather. Studies have found that, after an El Niño event, diseases caused by mosquito bites, such as malaria, affect more people in India and parts of South America. El Niño's rains make conditions suitable for the spread of these insects. Also, El Niño-caused droughts lead to fewer crops, so people have less to eat. Hunger can cause unrest and sometimes even wars.

HOW EL NIÑO WORKS

NORMAL YEAR

ASIA

PACIFIC OCEAN

NORTH AMERICA

TRADE WINDS BLOW WEST: WARM WATERS GATHER IN THE WESTERN PACIFIC

AUSTRALIA

SOUTH AMERICA

COLD WATERS ALONG SOUTH AMERICAN COAST

EL NIÑO YEAR

ASIA

PACIFIC OCEAN

NORTH AMERICA

WARMER WINTER IN THE NORTH; MORE RAIN IN THE SOUTH

TRADE WINDS WEAKEN: WARM WATERS MOVE EASTWARD

AUSTRALIA

SOUTH AMERICA

EL NIÑO MEANS "THE BOY CHILD" IN SPANISH. IT WAS NAMED BY FISHERMEN WHO NOTICED IT CAME AROUND CHRISTMAS, WHEN PEOPLE CELEBRATE JESUS'S BIRTH.

MORE FREAKY PHENOMENA

There are so many more freaky weather events and stories to learn about. For example, on June 3, 1980, seven tornadoes touched down in and around a single city—Grand Island, Nebraska. In February 2017, parts of Oklahoma experienced a day that got as hot as 99°F (37°C). Just 3 days later, it snowed. And in March 2018, dust from Africa blew over Eastern Europe, mixed with clouds, and created orange snow!

If there's one thing you can count on, it's that the weather will get weird at times. It seems that all the weather technology in the world can't predict some strange events. Maybe someday you'll become the meteorologist who discovers a new way of making better weather predictions!

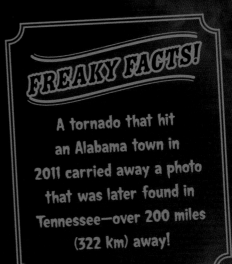

FREAKY FACTS!

A tornado that hit an Alabama town in 2011 carried away a photo that was later found in Tennessee—over 200 miles (322 km) away!

THERE ARE OTHER EXPLANATIONS FOR ODD-COLORED SNOW. WATERMELON SNOW IS SNOW THAT IS COLORED PINK OR RED BY A CERTAIN KIND OF ALGA!

STRANGE SPORTS WEATHER

Weird weather can even impact sports. This was true of the football game between the Buffalo Bills and the New England Patriots on December 28, 2008. The winds were so strong at times—as much as 75 miles (121 km) per hour—that they tilted the goalposts. The posts had to be straightened four times. The wind also meant the teams' quarterbacks didn't throw as much as they would have normally. Wacky weather really can affect life in many ways!

GLOSSARY

depression: an area on a surface that is lower than other parts

drought: a long period of very dry weather

evaporate: to change from a liquid to a gas

hexagon: a flat shape that has six angles and six sides

humidity: moisture in the air

impair: to make something weaker or worse

phenomena: extraordinary events

predict: to guess what will happen in the future based on facts or knowledge

saturated: full of water

technology: tools, machines, or ways to do things that use the latest discoveries to fix problems or meet needs

tornado: a violent and destructive storm in which powerful winds move around a central point

trade winds: winds that blow almost constantly to the west and toward the equator

wavelength: the distance from one wave of energy to another as it is traveling from one point to another point

FOR MORE INFORMATION

BOOKS

Bright, Michael. *Weather Explained*. New York, NY: Rosen Publishing, 2015.

Coss, Lauren. *Weird-But-True Facts About Weather*. Mankato, MN: Child's World, 2013.

Leet, Karen M. *This Book Might Blow You Away: A Collection of Amazing Weather Trivia*. North Mankato, MN: Capstone Press, 2013.

WEBSITES

30 Freaky Facts About Weather
natgeokids.com/za/discover/geography/physical-geography/30-freaky-facts-about-weather/
Discover facts about weather to share with your friends.

Cloud Facts for Kids
sciencekids.co.nz/sciencefacts/weather/clouds.html
Haven't gotten enough of clouds? This website will tell you everything you need to know!

INDEX